Railways of
East Anglia

1955–1980

JOHN JENNISON & TONY SHEFFIELD

Ian Allan
PUBLISHING

First published 2013

ISBN 978 0 7110 3654 3

© John Jennison and Tony Sheffield 2013

Published by Ian Allan Publishing

an imprint of Ian Allan Publishing Ltd, Hersham, Surrey KT12 4RG.
Printed in Estonia

Visit the Ian Allan Publishing website at www.ianallanpublishing.com

FRONT COVER Stratford-allocated 'B17/6' No 61654 *Sunderland* stands in the platform at Melton Constable in 1956 with an eastbound train for Yarmouth; the locomotive would move to Norwich in the summer of 1958. Melton was the junction for the two branch lines to Cromer and Norwich and its two goods yards played an important role in freight working on the former Midland & Great Northern Joint line. Engine changing and train splitting manoeuvres were a feature of operation at this junction. The station was an island platform which could accommodate 12 coaches at either side. The up platform had an intermediate locomotive release crossover complete with mandatory facing point lock, which is just visible in the foreground, and thus it could handle two trains simultaneously. *Colour-Rail.com [J. Cramp]*

BACK COVER Class 37 No 37026 approaches Norwich station on 2 September 1978 as it passes Norwich Thorpe Junction signalbox. Built as No D6726 and allocated to Stratford from September 1961 until April 1966 when it moved to March, it returned to Stratford briefly before going back to March in October 1977. It was renumbered as 37026 in February 1974 and 37320 in July 1986 when in Scotland; withdrawn in January 1999. Crown Point Traction Maintenance depot would later be built on the sidings between the signalbox and the gas holder. *www.rail-online.co.uk*

LEFT Class 37 No 37092 on 5 August 1978 at Great Bealings on the line between Ipswich and Lowestoft. Built in February 1963 as No D6792 and renumbered in February 1974, it was allocated to the North Eastern Region at various depots but by the date of this photograph it had moved to March. It was withdrawn in July 1999. The station was shut in September 1956 although both the station building and platforms still survive today. *www.rail-online.co.uk*

PAGE 1 'Britannia' No 70013 *Oliver Cromwell* is at Stowmarket in October 1959. The 'Britannias' revolutionised the Great Eastern express services when introduced in 1951, providing one of the best regular interval steam services in the country. *Oliver Cromwell* was the last of the class to remain in BR service and took a leading role in the 1968 end of steam workings before its preservation as part of the National Collection. *Colour-Rail.com*

Introduction

The last Ian Allan colour book on East Anglia was published as long ago as 1997 and covered the steam era. In this volume we will be looking at the quarter century from 1955 up to 1980, a period which saw the phasing out of steam, the introduction of the first generation of diesel traction and the beginnings of the era of standardisation which preceded privatisation in the 1990s. We have attempted to provide a good balance across this timespan, by geographical area, by motive power and between main and rural lines. We hope you enjoy the journey from ex-Great Eastern Railway (GER) steam via green diesels and diesel multiple-units (DMUs) into that oft-neglected early blue period, putting the brakes on as we enter the TOPS era and drifting gently up to the buffers in 1980.

Before we embark on our trip, we need to define with a moderate degree of precision what we mean by East Anglia, and in particular where that may differ from the accepted definition of the counties of Norfolk, Suffolk and Cambridgeshire plus eastern parts of Essex. From the railway angle, which seems to make more sense for our immediate purpose, we are essentially looking at the area covered by the old Great Eastern Railway, plus a couple of 'intruding' lines at the borders of its fiefdom in the shape of the Midland & Joint Railway (M&GNJR) and the London, Tilbury & Southend Railway (LTSR).

From Liverpool Street there was a steep climb out to Bethnal Green where the tracks divided, the line which ran straight ahead going through Essex into Suffolk and Norfolk and the one to the left going north towards Cambridge and then on across the Fens through March and Ely to the North Norfolk Coast at Hunstanton. There were several important junctions on the Essex line starting at Shenfield for the Southend line, at Witham to Braintree, Dunmow and Bishop's Stortford to the left and to the right to Maldon East. Colchester had junctions for Walton-on-the-Naze and Clacton-on-Sea and Brightlingsea and further north was Manningtree with the triangle which allowed train movements in all directions from Harwich and Parkeston Quay. Into Suffolk, Ipswich was a major junction where the main lines again divided, running almost due north to Norfolk and Norwich, and to the east for the East Suffolk main line with branches to Felixstowe at Westerfield, Framlingham and Snape at Wickham Market and Saxmundham for the Aldeburgh branch. At Beccles was a three-way junction: to the west the line ran across country to Tivetshall on the Ipswich-to-Norwich line, to the east for Lowestoft whilst that which ran northwards went to Yarmouth. The Norwich line out of Ipswich passed through Stowmarket to a junction at Haughley where a line branched westwards to Bury St Edmunds and on to Cambridge via Newmarket, whilst the line to Norwich passed through Diss before reaching the city.

Our journey begins at Liverpool Street, stopping firstly at Stratford where we will linger for a while in the 1960s to have a look at a number of those short-lived early diesels which were rarely captured in colour, especially the shunting engines. As we gather speed we will firstly go northwards into Cambridgeshire before retracing our steps to Stratford and then heading eastwards.

By the mid-1950s the Great Eastern had seen a revolution in its principal main line services with the 'Britannia' Pacifics comfortably ensconced in one of the best regular interval steam services in the country. Most of the suburban and branch lines were still steam operated, with the exception of the Liverpool Street-Shenfield route which was electrified in the late 1940s. The 1954 British Railways Modernisation Plan was to set in motion a period of rapid change which, by the end of September 1962, saw the complete elimination of steam traction in the former Great Eastern area and its replacement by the first-generation diesels and further suburban electrification. East Anglia was one of the first areas of the country to experience this revolution as DMUs took over rural lines, and English Electric Type 4s, Brush Type 2s, English Electric Type 3s and diesel shunters replaced the 'Britannias', 'B1s' and the other long-serving steam classes. In the late-1960s there was a second wave with Brush Type 4 Class 47s displacing the Class 40s and some of the weakest diesel designs followed the steam engines to the scrapyard as short-distance freight traffic declined.

'N7/4' 0-6-2T No 69621 is at Liverpool Street with a Quint-art articulated suburban set on the 'Jazz' service on 27 August 1960. The Enfield and Chingford services were taken over by electric units three months later. When it was withdrawn in September 1962, No 69621 was destined to become the only preserved 'N7' and was the last engine to be built at Stratford Works. Designed by Hill, the 'N7/4s' were rebuilt in the 1940s with round-top boilers, although they retained short travel valves. The GER ran the most intensive steam-worked services in the world. The nickname 'Jazz' arose because of the coloured bands used to identify the different classes in the coaching stock sets. The operation was extremely slick, especially during the rush hours. After an incoming train arrived the fireman would uncouple the engine and another engine would couple-up at the other end and within minutes the train would leave. The first engine would back out on the dock at the end of the platform, waiting for only 10 minutes or so for the next arrival, and the process would be repeated. *Colour-Rail.com*

The 1970s brought standardisation to the British Rail network and the Corporate Rail Blue period brought a dull drabness to the scene as locomotives, DMUs and even electrical multiple-units (EMUs) were painted in all-over blue and soon faded to a semi-matt finish. As ever there were pockets of independence, led by Stratford which by 1977 had started painting silver roofs on its best Class 47s and even unofficially named one 'Great Eastern' in 1978 until the authorities found out. East Anglia was home to many Class 03 shunters throughout the period, and they could be found all over the region from Stratford (for the docks), to Ipswich, Colchester and Kings Lynn (again for the docks and officially March machines). However, it was Norwich, which was the bastion of the class, with all its shunting allocation being the little 204hp '03s' until the first '08s' arrived in the spring of 1976. Even then the staff still preferred their '03s'. The official reason for the preference was due to their higher speed, allowing movement between outstations without causing disruption to other traffic, but all other regions seemed to manage!

It is easy to forget the EMUs that plied their trade out of Liverpool Street. The electrification was started by the London & North Eastern Railway (LNER) and the earliest units were of a plain 1948 design which was made worse when painted in drab all-over blue which was little better than the overall dark green which preceded it. The more glamorous Clacton units were originally delivered in maroon and were the only EMUs to escape the all-over blue livery, being outshopped in Inter-city blue and grey, although they lost some of their style when the wrap-around windows were removed. Even easier to forget were the non-electrified lines that Stratford served with an aged fleet of 'first-generation' DMUs. The journey from Stratford (Low Level) to Silvertown was not one undertaken by many tourists, but was a fascinating trip in a Cravens unit for the discerning railway enthusiast.

To the north, the huge Whitemoor yards at March saw a large decline in traffic over the period covered. Once there had been a constant flow of coal trains from the Derbyshire and Yorkshire coalfields routed via the Great Northern & Great Eastern Joint Railway (GN&GEJR) joint line to March (where they changed locomotives) and onward via Cambridge to Temple Mills yard and the capital; in the opposite direction agricultural produce was sent north. By the 1970s the capital's need for coal had declined and the traffic faded away. Whitemoor was still an important yard for traffic from the Midlands to the East, most arriving via Peterborough, but it was in heavy decline, weeds took over and the first phase of rationalisation loomed. March TMD (as it was then known) provided motive power for the entire East Anglia fleet, and standardisation really had taken hold with Classes 37 and especially 31 dominating both freight and passenger traffic and March engines were outstabled throughout the area. Through traffic from the Midlands and the North still brought variety and Classes 40 and 47 often worked in, especially on the growing Freightliner traffic to Felixstowe. London Midland Region (LMR) Class 25s worked through, usually in pairs, to Norwich and Yarmouth on passenger services, mainly at weekends, but later, upon conversion of the Birmingham to Norwich services from DMUs to locomotive-hauled services, they were occasionally substituted for the regular March Class 31 motive power. March TMD was a magnet for enthusiasts; upon entering the depot you were immediately confronted with the overflow stabling sidings, at weekends full of locomotives that had brought traffic to Whitemoor and would not return until Monday.

This book is primarily about photographs and to produce it we have drawn on the collections of Rail-online, Colour-Rail, Geoff Corner and the Transport Treasury. As far as we can, we have selected photographs which have not previously been published and we would particularly like to thank Andrew Harvey-Jones who took a large number of pictures in the area between 1975 and 1980, at a time when few photographers were recording the contemporary scene.

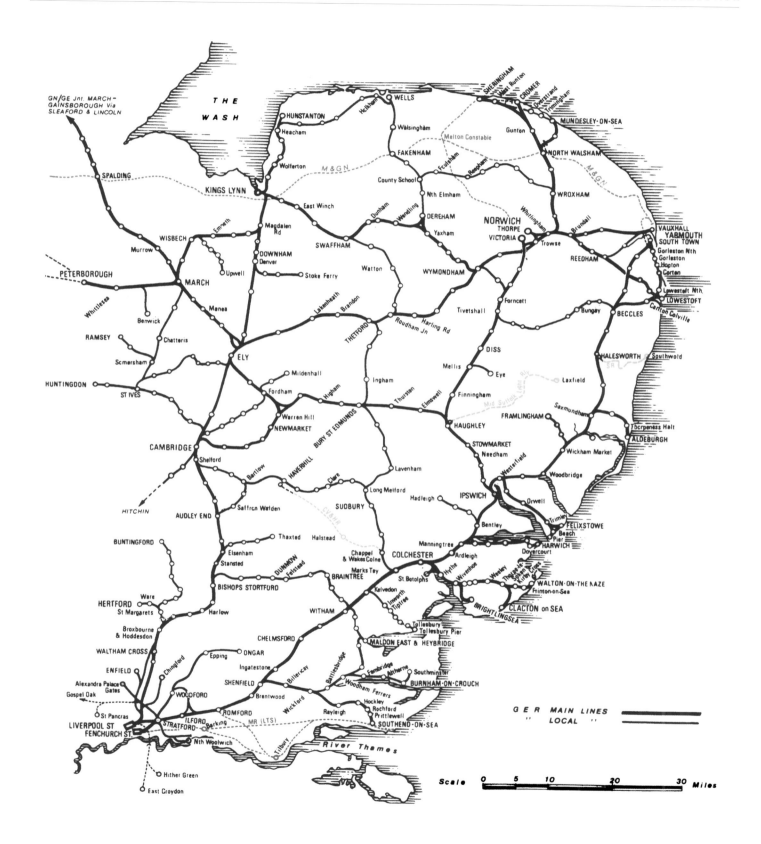

Locally allocated 'B17/6' No 61652 *Darlington* is heading south out of Cambridge station on 4 May 1959 with what is undoubtedly a Liverpool Street service. The two station pilots, a pair of 204hp Drewry shunters, are coupled nose to nose but unlike in later years do not have match runner trucks to activate the train detection equipment. In the 1970s there would still be a pair at the station, but they would stable near the scissors crossover in the middle of the long platform. Sadly, *Darlington* would only remain in service until September 1959 so this scene would soon be lost forever. *Colour-Rail.com*

Liverpool Street

ABOVE No 68619 was repainted in September 1959 in GER royal blue with red lining and the Great Eastern crest on the bunker below the number and became a familiar sight on Liverpool Street pilot duties. Unfortunately it would not last much longer after this August 1961 picture because the 'J69/1' was withdrawn at the end of October and cut up at Stratford, its place of birth. *Colour-Rail.com*

FACING PAGE TOP When the 'Britannia' Pacifics arrived on the Great Eastern lines in 1951 they revolutionised the express service, providing a fast regular interval service from London to Norwich via Ipswich and in 1953 via Cambridge. No 70002 *Geoffrey Chaucer* stands at the cramped servicing area just by the turntable at Liverpool Street in late 1959. The close proximity of Broad Street (at the higher level) can be seen by the signal in the background. The locomotive has modified handrails but was not fitted with the Automatic Warning System (AWS) until February 1960. No 70002 was originally at Stratford but was transferred to Norwich in March 1959 along with the other Stratford 'Britannias' because of a severe shortage of maintenance staff at the London shed. After moving again to March in June 1961 it left for the LMR at Carlisle Kingmoor after a period in store between July and December 1963. *www.rail-online.co.uk*

FACING PAGE BOTTOM In September 1959 the British Railways Design Panel recommended various experimental liveries for the trials of visibility tests to try and improve lineside safety with the new diesel and electric traction. Tests were to be carried out on the GE line using several DMUs and EMUs and three Brush Type 2s. Two were selected from the production line at Loughborough and specially treated, No D5579 in bronze yellow with light grey lining bands and No D5578 in electric blue, with the third in the standard green livery. The tests took place at Alresford between Colchester and Clacton on 28 June 1960, although the locomotives went into traffic at the start of the year. No D5578 was used in lieu of an LMR ac electric locomotive and was given a white roof to replicate the appearance as closely as possible. The results showed the blue was an improvement on the green, but the bronze was poor in sunlight and not much better than the green – contrary to expectations before the tests. No D5578, pictured on the turntable at Liverpool Street in March 1960, kept the blue for several years although it was repainted green before Rail Blue was introduced. *Colour-Rail.com*

ABOVE The drabness of the BR green livery and the dreary 'East side' of Liverpool Street (Platforms 11-18) are evident in this view of three EMUs at the station in early 1961. It was not surprising that experiments were already underway to improve the visibility of diesel and electric traction for trackside workers. 'AM4' unit No 019 on the left has a wooden patch over the second pane of its route indicator panel; its destination blind is not in use. It was on loan together with unit Nos 018 and 020 from the London Midland Region, having been built for the Crewe-Manchester and Liverpool services. It has a modicum of lining, unlike the two Eastern Region units. In the centre with a Gidea Park destination blind is unit No 054, a 1949 'AM6' Liverpool St-Shenfield three-car set converted from dc operation. On the right is a 1956 'AM7' Liverpool St-Shenfield three-car set, No 122, with its blind showing Southend Victoria. *www.rail-online.co.uk*

FACING PAGE TOP At the end of the 1960s the second generation of mainline diesels arrived on the Great Eastern in the form of the Brush Type 4. These took over the principal express work from the lower-powered English Electric Type 4s. No 1524 waits to leave Liverpool Street on 8 June 1971. It was built in June 1963 and originally allocated to Finsbury Park for the GNR main line, moved to Sheffield Tinsley in May 1968 and by the time of this photograph was allocated to Stratford, where it was based from February 1970 until October 1971 when it moved to York. *www.rail-online.co.uk*

FACING PAGE BOTTOM The LNER decided to electrify the Liverpool Street to Shenfield section of the Colchester main line before World War 2. Civil engineering works began in the 1930s but the war intervened and the work was not completed until 1949; the electrification was extended to Chelmsford and Southend (Victoria) in 1956. On the right of this photograph taken at Liverpool Street in the late 1970s is unit No 039, a Liverpool Street-Shenfield three-car set built in 1949 (later Class 306). They had sliding doors unlike the later Great Eastern units. The sockets to hold the multiple-unit cables are prominent on the cab front. The other unit is No 110, a GE outer suburban four-car set built in 1956 when the line to Southend was electrified. These took a step backwards, reverting to a slam-door design similar to the Southern Region (SR) 'EPB' stock built at the same time; they became Class 307 under TOPS. Both types were originally built for 1,500 volts dc operation and were converted to 25,000 volts ac in 1960. The route indicator panel on unit No 110 has been modified to the four-character type; No 039 still has its original two-character pattern with which it was fitted when converted to ac operation at Stratford works; the 'AM7s' were dealt with at Eastleigh. *www.rail-online.co.uk*

Class 37 No 37060 arrives at Liverpool Street on 11 August 1979 with a train from King's Lynn. It was built as D6760 in October 1962 and renumbered in March 1974, and was based in the North East at Thornaby and Immingham before moving to Stratford in October 1976. *www.rail-online.co.uk*

Stratford

Stratford looked after many different early diesel classes, such as No D2954 seen there on 30 April 1961. The 0-4-0 diesel-mechanical locomotive, originally numbered 11504 and renumbered in November 1960, had a 153hp Gardner 6L3 engine and was built by Andrew Barclay at Kilmarnock. Stratford was its first shed in February 1956 and it left there in April 1965 for Newton Heath. It then went to Holyhead in 1967 for use by William Wild & Sons Ltd on the Holyhead breakwater railway, where it was based until 1979. Amongst enthusiasts it became a celebrity locomotive when it was given the first number in the TOPS series, 01001 in 1974. *www.rail-online.co.uk*

FACING PAGE TOP Brush Type 2 No D5579 on 14 January 1962 at Stratford is still in the bronze yellow used for the visibility trials at Alresford in 1960. Surprisingly the blue-painted D5578 was deemed more successful because the bronze yellow did not show up well in bright light. Under the TOPS renumbering, D5579 became No 31161 in 1974 and No 31400 in May 1988 when it was reinstated following the repair of severe fire damage which had resulted in its initial withdrawal in March 1988. *www.rail-online.co.uk*

FACING PAGE BOTTOM Thompson 'B1' 4-6-0 No 61362 is seen on 4 November 1962 at Stratford with Sentinel 0-4-0 Dept No 39. The Sentinels were used for shunting in areas such as docks where tight radius curves had to be negotiated. It was built in 1926 as No 8401 and worked first at Lowestoft CE Depot, then Norwich and finally Cambridge from 1955 for working at Chesterton Junction; it was withdrawn in April 1963. No 61362 was a local Stratford locomotive most of its life, with only a brief spell away at Parkeston in 1959-60. It was withdrawn in September 1962 and cut up at Doncaster three months later. *www.rail-online.co.uk*

ABOVE This 204hp 0-4-0 diesel-electric locomotive, No D2999 pictured on 9 August 1964 at Stratford, was one of Brush Traction's stock locomotives, produced speculatively to try to gain industrial orders. Built by Beyer-Peacock at Gorton in 1958, it was loaned to BR, allocated to Stratford and trialled at Mile End Goods Yard. It was purchased by British Railways in September 1960 and was repainted in BR green in March 1961. It was withdrawn in April 1967. *www.rail-online.co.uk*

ABOVE The first North British Locomotive Company (NBL) Type 1 No D8400 is at its Stratford home in September 1964. It looks very smart, complete with new yellow warning panel, and as Stratford continued the steam tradition of providing a clean locomotive as Liverpool Street pilot, this may have been its next duty. Built in May 1958, No D8400 lasted just 10 years before withdrawal under the National Traction Plan. *www.rail-online.co.uk*

FACING PAGE TOP Ten Type 1 800hp single-ended diesels were ordered from the North British Locomotive Company under the British Railways Modernisation Pilot Scheme, the design following the LMS Bo-Bo prototype No 10800. No D8402, seen at Stratford in 1967, entered service there on 16 July 1958 and with its classmates stayed there until the rationalisation of diesel classes from 1967 onwards. The class failed the selection criteria on two counts: they were unreliable and non-standard. D8402 was withdrawn on 3 July 1968 after being stored from the start of the year. It was moved to Cohens of Kettering in February 1969 and cut-up there by the end of November. *www.rail-online.co.uk*

ABOVE Diesel-hydraulics were frequent visitors to the GE lines, primarily to Temple Mills Yard on cross-London freight services, but also to Stratford for tyre turning. North British Type 2, later Class 22, No D6356 was there in April 1967. Note the tail lamp that suggests it has probably been hauled to Stratford from Old Oak Common for this service. D6356 was allocated to Old Oak from October 1964. Withdrawn at the end of December 1968, it was cut-up at Cashmore's, Newport, in mid-1969. *www.rail-online.co.uk*

RIGHT A familiar sight at Stratford for over a decade, the milk trains made up of six-wheeled tanks originated from the West Country and supplied the United Dairies bottling plant at Ilford up until 1978 when it closed. British Thomson-Houston (BTH) Type 1 No 8201 is handling the returning empties as it is heading west through Stratford station toward the Channelsea sidings curve and hence the North London line. These locomotives worked the traffic usually from Kensington Olympia and were regular performers on the North London line right up to their demise. No 8201 was one of the Pilot Scheme batch of 10 BTH Type 1 Bo-Bos. It was built by the Yorkshire Engine Company at Sheffield, using Clayton-built bogies and superstructure, and delivered to the London Midland Region at Devons Road, Bow, on 17 February 1958. It was transferred to Stratford in November 1959 and withdrawn from there in March 1971. After storage at Ipswich until January 1972 it was taken to Crewe Works for scrapping. *www.rail-online.co.uk*

ABOVE With experimental flashing lights, No D5553 was ahead of its time when pictured at Stratford in July 1967. These warning lights were fitted to four Brush Type 2 and four English Electric Type 3 locomotives at Stratford depot in April/May 1966 for evaluation in service trials on the Eastern Region. The lamps had clear glass and flashed alternately left and right. D5553 moved away from Stratford in March 1970 and moved around the country both north and south before returning as 31135 in 1987 and again in 1989. *www.rail-online.co.uk*

RIGHT A 30A stalwart, Brush Type 2 No D5506 is at Stratford in the early 1970s with a train of 'Airfix' Esso tank wagons heading for the North London line at Stratford station. The back of the shed is visible in the distance. The locomotive remained at Stratford all its life, being withdrawn as No 31006 in January 1980. *www.rail-online.co.uk*

FACING PAGE TOP English Electric Type 1 Nos D8030-33 were transferred from the LMR in September 1968, having moved down from Scotland to the Nottingham D16 Division three months earlier. No D8032 as seen at Stratford in around 1970 in the curious hybrid livery of old-style serif numbers but with the new BR double arrow symbol. The cut-out in the cab side was to allow a tablet catcher to be fitted for use on the single lines in Scotland but few of the class were ever fitted with the equipment. The English Electric Type 1s were drafted into Stratford's allocation to replace the North British and BTH Type 1 classes which were being withdrawn. However, they worked side by side with the BTHs for about three years as the survivors of that class had reached an acceptable level of performance. When traffic declined the English Electrics were transferred away, the last going north in the autumn of 1971. *www.rail-online.co.uk*

FACING PAGE BOTTOM Two BTH Type 1s are parked in the middle of Stratford depot in the early spring of 1971 in front of the pioneer Brush Type 2 D5500. Traffic flows have changed and the Type 1s have become surplus to requirements and await a decision on their fate: No 8221 has a blue TOPS panel, no 'D' and still has its BR crest, unlike 8242 behind which is in green with a BR double arrow. None of the class was repainted into

blue yet several acquired double arrows. Both were withdrawn on 28 March and almost immediately stored at the closed Ipswich steam shed before moving to Crewe Works for cutting-up in October. *www.rail-online.co.uk*

ABOVE A 'Toffee Apple' Class 31 is photographed inside Stratford Works on 16 September 1978. Nicknamed 'Toffee Apples' from the shape of the driver's control key, which had to be taken from cab to cab when changing ends, these Pilot Scheme locomotives were non-standard in having electro-magnetic multiple-working control equipment designated by the red spots above the buffers and were limited to 80mph. No 31017 was built in 1958 as D5517 and was always a Stratford locomotive, apart from a very brief spell at March in 1970. It was renumbered in April 1974 and withdrawn in May 1980. *www.rail-online.co.uk*

The Cambridge line, Ely, Wisbech and branches

ABOVE '03' shunter No 03168 is seen at Stratford on 22 March 1980. It was built as D2168 in November 1960, and spent its first decade on Humberside at Hull Alexandra Docks and Dairycoates. It was transferred to Stratford in April 1971 and renumbered in April 1974. The Stratford 204hp shunters, as the drivers used to call them, were used in the remains of Poplar docks and as pilots in Stratford depot and works, but there always seemed more of them than were actually needed. No 03168 was withdrawn in August 1981 to be sent to Doncaster works for component recovery and dismantling, which occurred almost a year later. *www.rail-online.co.uk*

RIGHT Class 31 No 31176 on 28 April 1980 is at Hackney Downs with a Cambridge-Liverpool Street service on the Cambridge line out of Bethnal Green. The first few miles out of the capital were hard work for these low-powered locomotives and timing was tight. No 31176 was originally No D5597, renumbered in March 1974. It was allocated to March from October 1978 until January 1982. *www.rail-online.co.uk*

FACING PAGE TOP BR Sulzer Type 2 No D5062 is photographed in May 1960 at Elsenham, between Bishop's Stortford and Cambridge. This was typical employment for the class on a mixed parcels train; the second vehicle is an ex-LMS motor car van which found use as a general parcels vehicle despite its limited side door capacity. No D5062 went new to March in January 1960, but soon moved away to the LMR at Longsight in October of that year. It became No 24060 in March 1974 and was withdrawn in October 1975. *Colour-Rail.com; M Thompson*

FACING PAGE BOTTOM The driver climbs into the cab of North British Type 1 D8401 from the weed-grown platform at Buntingford in 1965. Increased car ownership allowed commuters to try Bishop's Stortford and the Great Northern stations from which a much faster service ran to King's Cross, which was far more convenient for the West End offices.

Passenger services had limped on and despite spirited public objections and a proposal to reduce costs by introducing a railbus, they finally ceased on 16 November 1964. A freight service was retained to Hadham, Standon and Buntingford until 17 September 1965. Barely four months after the complete closure of the line, the track was lifted. No D8401 was out of use by January 1968 and stored at Stratford until formally withdrawn at the end of September. *www.rail-online.co.uk*

ABOVE Liverpool Street-bound Class 305 EMU 404 is seen on 13 March 1980 at Northumberland Park with the London Transport depot in the background. These three-car units were built at York in 1960 for the opening of the Liverpool Street to Chingford and Enfield services. *www.rail-online.co.uk*

FACING PAGE TOP Ex-North Eastern Railway (NER) 'G5' 0-4-4T No 67279 in June 1956 is at Audley End with a Bartlow train. The station served the small village of Wendens Ambo and the nearby town of Saffron Walden, and was named after the manor of Audley End. The two-coach train is formed of elderly ex-GER vehicles converted by the LNER in 1924 to push and pull sets for the Palace Gates to Severn Sisters service and transferred to Cambridge in July 1951 along with the NER 'G5s' (which came south to Stratford after the war), outbased for the Saffron Waldon service. They worked until worn out in November 1956. *Colour-Rail.com [G W Powell]*

FACING PAGE BOTTOM A Waggon und Maschinenbau railbus is shown here in 1964 at Haverhill. They were originally used on Cambridge-Mildenhall, Audley End-Bartlow, Bartlow-Mark's Tey, Witham-Braintree and Witham-Maldon services. Four of the five railbuses were in use each day on a cyclic diagram working each of these services, stabling overnight at Braintree, Maldon East, Saffron Walden and finally Cambridge for maintenance the following day. They were quickly withdrawn from the Witham-Braintree and Witham-Maldon services because they had insufficient luggage capacity. *www.rail-online.co.uk*

ABOVE A Waggon und Maschinenbau railbus is at Saffron Walden in 1963. Introduced in April 1958, Nos E79660-4 arrived on the line from 7 July and were stationed at Cambridge, but were left overnight at Saffron Walden until refuelling or repairs were needed. At first failures were common and initially an 'N7' and push-pull set was kept to substitute. Once they had settled down they became very reliable although they were unpopular, partly because of their ride quality but mainly due to the limited seating capacity (56 passengers), especially for the peak commuting times. Some of the 78 season ticket holders to London, unhappy with the service and missing their first class accommodation, drove to Audley End. Note that one buffer had a flat head and the other a convex one, apparently to assist smooth negotiation of curves when coupled. *www.rail-online.co.uk*

LEFT German-built Waggon und Maschinenbau railbus No E79961 departs from the Saffron Walden platform at Audley End in September 1963. The Beeching Report published in March 1963 had recommended closure of the branch and a survey taken the following month revealed that a daily average of 266 persons alighted at Audley End, mainly from Saffron Walden. A bus service was the obvious outcome and Premier Travel initiated its route 59 on 7 September 1964, the day of closure. The GER down starting signal, gas lamps, seats and waiting room survived to the end on the Audley End branch platform although there was some modernisation on the main line platforms by this time. Note that ballast wagons are stored in the siding. *www.rail-online.co.uk*

ABOVE Locally allocated 'B2' 4-6-0 No 61632 *Belvoir Castle* waits in the down bay at Cambridge in April 1958 with a local. This locomotive would, for five months from 22 September 1958, become *Royal Sovereign* and carry the plates from No 61671 as the Royal Engine, although there is no record of it actually doing any royal duties. The fireman is on the top of the tender attending to the coal; this tender was once attached to Gresley 'P1' 2-8-2 No 2394. The crimson and cream livery looked good when clean and went well with the green of the passenger locomotives. *Colour-Rail.com [P H Wells]*

LEFT A Class 108 DMU is seen at Old North Road in October 1960 with original speed whiskers. This was the second Derby 'Lightweight' design with low-density seating and formed in two-, three- or four-car sets. The headcode destination states 'Cambridge' and it has just three more stops before reaching the end of its journey. Old North Road was a station on the Oxford to Cambridge 'Varsity' Line which served the small village of Longstowe near Bourn in Cambridgeshire. As its name suggests, the station was located on the eastern side of the Old North Road – a Roman road which linked Lincoln with London. Opened in 1862 by the Bedford & Cambridge Railway, later part of the London & North Western Railway (LNWR), as part of its line from Bedford, the station was located in a rural area and saw little passenger traffic; it closed together with the line in 1968. *www.rail-online.co.uk*

ABOVE No E51274, a Class 105 Cravens two-car unit in its original green livery with cream speed whiskers, is seen at Fordham, Cambridgeshire, in the early 1960s. The station served the Bury St Edmunds-Ely main line, and the Cambridge-Mildenhall branch. Following closure in September 1965, the yard and buildings were used in turn by a roofing/scaffolding contractor and as a waste management depot. They are currently unoccupied, awaiting redevelopment. *www.rail-online.co.uk*

FACING PAGE TOP A Class 105 Cravens DMU is photographed at Mildenhall Suffolk, the terminus of the Cambridge to Mildenhall line which closed in 1962. The two large front windows in these units gave a neat appearance and good forward vision for both driver and passengers. They incorporated features from the contemporary Mark 1 coaches such as sliding toplight windows, door droplights and metal luggage racks, all of which picked up vibrations from the engines and created a significant rattle. The single bolster bogies did not help and when worn were prone to 'hunting'. *www.rail-online.co.uk*

FACING PAGE BOTTOM On 29 July 1960 Cambridge-allocated 'B1' 4-6-0 No 61363 rolls into Ely with steam to spare past the faded GER starting signal complete with its short cast-iron finial. The signalbox displays the blue and cream BR(E) livery. *www.rail-online.co.uk*

ABOVE Brush Type 2 No D5550 rests in the spring sunshine at Stoke Ferry in March 1965. Stoke Ferry was the terminus of a 7¼-mile branch line from Denver, on the Ely-Kings Lynn main line, opened in August 1882. It closed to passengers in September 1930 and to all traffic in 1965. No D5550 was allocated to Ipswich when new in September 1959 and stayed there until transferred to Tinsley in October 1965. It became 31132 in March 1974 under the TOPS renumbering. *www.rail-online.co.uk*

ABOVE Drewry 204hp diesel shunter No 11101 in July 1955 is seen at Outwell on the Wisbech & Upwell Tramway. Two of these locomotives were introduced on the tramway in 1952, replacing the 'J70' steam tram engines. No 11101 was renumbered as D2201 in December 1961. The line provided inspiration for Toby the Tram Engine in the Rev W. Awdry's 'Thomas the Tank Engine' books. It was opened in 1883 by the Great Eastern Railway to carry agricultural produce. Although called a tramway, in many ways it more closely resembled a conventional railway line, although it was operated under Board of Trade tram rules which demanded speed restrictions and the fitting of cowcatchers and skirts over the wheels. The line closed to passengers in 1927 but goods services lasted until May 1966, remaining in the hands of the Drewries until the end. *Colour-Rail.com [J J Davis]*

FACING PAGE TOP Drewry shunter, later BR Class 04, No D2201 is photographed in the early 1960s on the Wisbech & Upwell Tramway. D2201 moved to March for use on the tramway in March 1952 before ending its days as a Crewe Works shunter from September 1966 to April 1968. Incoming traffic on the line was principally coal, with outgoing traffic consisting of vegetables, fruit, and, in later years, flowers. *www.rail-online.co.uk*

FACING PAGE BOTTOM 'D16/3' 4-4-0 No 62610 is seen in 1958 at Wisbech East. The station was opened in 1848 and provided connections to March, Watlington and St Ives, as well as Upwell via the Wisbech & Upwell Tramway. It closed in 1968 and no trace of it remains today. The 'D16' was allocated to King's Lynn from October 1957 until withdrawn on 1 January 1959. *Colour-Rail.com*

Stratford – North Woolwich

Class 105 Cravens Driving Trailer Composite Lavatory (DTCL) No E56122 and Driving Motor Brake Second (DMBS) No E50363 pass Stratford Southern signalbox on 25 May 1978 with the 13.41 Stratford to North Woolwich service. The DMU appears to have been in works recently and its original headcode panels have been plated over. The easternmost section of the North London line between Richmond and North Woolwich opened as the Eastern Counties & Thames Junction Railway in 1846/7 between Stratford and North Woolwich. On 10 December 2006 it was closed to allow building between Stratford and Canning Town of the Docklands Light Railway line to Stratford International. *Paul G. Bennett © TOPticl Digital Memories*

ABOVE Class 104 Nos E50543, E59220 and E50547 are on the 17.34 North Woolwich to Stratford at Silvertown on 29 August 1972. These Birmingham Railway Carriage & Wagon Company (BRC&W) low-density units were built in 1957 and were generally successful, some surviving into the 1990s despite being excluded from the 1974 refurbishment programme. The unit still has its two-character headcode blind in use. Silvertown was opened in 1863 by the Eastern Counties & Thames Junction Railway, with two tracks and two platforms. A decline in use of the line led to its singling in 1980 with one platform to serve trains in both directions. In railway circles Silvertown is best known for the mechanical lubricators used on hundreds of steam engines which were manufactured by Messrs Gresham & Craven for Silvertown Lubricants Ltd of Minoco Wharf, West Silvertown.
Paul G. Bennett © TOPticl Digital Memories

RIGHT Gresley 'N7' 0-6-2T No 69646 on 24 August 1962 is at North Woolwich. It was condemned less than a month later on 16 September when the services were taken over by DMUs, the last eight working 'N7s' being withdrawn *en-bloc*. Note the engine from the incoming train at the buffer stops, a BR Clas 2MT 2-6-0. From the 1980s only one track of the double-track line was used through the Connaught Tunnel under the Royal Docks. The station building at North Woolwich was closed and replaced by a minimalist entrance and passenger shelter on the south side. In 1985 the line from North Woolwich was electrified on the third-rail system with the service running round north London to Richmond, and is now known as the London Overground. *www.rail-online.co.uk*

Gresley 'N7' 0-6-2T No 69718 on 9 May 1960 is at North Woolwich. Adopted as a LNER 'group standard' class and allocated initially to Ardsley, like all of the class it soon migrated to home territory, moving to Stratford. It had a month-long visit to King's Lynn in the summer of 1959 but soon returned home. Despite receiving a casual light overhaul at Stratford in April 1960, No 69718 was condemned in December of the same year. North Woolwich station opened in 1847 as the southern terminus of the Eastern Counties & Thames Junction Railway from Stratford. In 1962 diesel traction replaced steam and the service was cut back to Stratford with peak-hour trains to Tottenham Hale. The route became an extension of the North London line in 1979.
www.rail-online.co.uk

London, Tilbury and Southend

ABOVE '4MT' No 42502 on 14 October 1961 departs bunker first from Plaistow for Fenchurch Street past the former London, Tilbury & Southern Railway (LTSR) engine shed, now in industrial service for, rather ironically, Volkswagen. The shed had been made redundant by the opening of the new larger West Ham shed complete with a well-equipped fitting shop in 1912 and was immediately given over to wagon repairs. The three-cylinder version of the Stanier 2-6-4T was the mainstay of the LTSR passenger services from their introduction in 1934 until 1962. They replaced the 4-4-2Ts which were struggling to cope with loads up to 11 bogies. The third cylinder was chosen because it appeared to offer improved acceleration and reduced hammer blow over the two-cylinder equivalents; they were the only LMS 2-6-4Ts which could be started on full regulator in full gear on a dry rail. No 42502 was built in April 1934 and withdrawn in June 1962 along with the other remaining three-cylinder engines. It was always allocated to Shoeburyness. The LTSR line was electrified in 1960/1 and although electric services began in November 1961 it was not until June 1962 that steam traction ceased. *Colour-Rail.com*

FACING PAGE TOP Fairburn 2-6-4T No 42255 in 1962 is seen after arrival at Tilbury Riverside. Built in November 1946 and condemned in June 1962 on electrification, No 42255 was one of only five which stayed on the LTSR until the bitter end. No Stanier two-cylinder 2-6-4Ts were allocated to the line, only the later Fairburns and BR Standards. A batch of 20 of the former, Nos 42218-27/48-57, were transferred to Plaistow in 1947 from the LMS Central Division. The BR '80000' 2-6-4Ts arrived in 1953-5, releasing some of the Fairburns to Neasden to replace 'L1s'. No 42255 was transferred to Tilbury from Plaistow in October 1959. Tilbury had been a passenger ferry terminal since the early 20th century but declined after World War 2 and when the Dartford Tunnel opened in 1963 the passenger service was drastically reduced. Freight traffic was withdrawn from May 1968 and the passenger service in November 1992. *www.rail-online.co.uk*

FACING PAGE BOTTOM Class 302 EMU No 300 in the late-1970s is seen departing from Barking for Fenchurch Street. These four-car units were built in 1958 for the London, Tilbury & Southend line electrification and were originally known to railwaymen as 'LTS stock'. *www.rail-online.co.uk*

Essex

ABOVE Cravens Class 105 No E56143 is seen at Romford around 1975 in the former LT&SR platform used for the shuttle service to Upminster. The Upminster and Wickford destination blind was there to confuse unsuspecting passengers because there was never a DMU service connecting these two stations, and anyway all the patrons would be regular locals! The blind was probably a compromise as there were more locations than the roller blind could accommodate. Like most DMU-powered branches that were served by Stratford-allocated units, the Romford to Upminster line was worked as a shuttle, the units only returning to the depot for fuel or servicing. *www.rail-online.co.uk*

FACING PAGE TOP A Stratford-based Class 116 is photographed at Braintree in September 1977. These Derby three-car suburban sets had cramped seating and slam-type doors to each bay, and no gangways. This example has plated-over route indicator boxes. Braintree was on the line from Witham to Bishops Stortford, off the Colchester main line; the route had been electrified the previous year. *www.rail-online.co.uk*

FACING PAGE BOTTOM 'J15' 0-6-0 No 65456 on 31 May 1958 crosses the timber trestle bridge at Wickham Bishops on the Maldon branch. The rear coach is a GER composite. The 'J15' was withdrawn in the following September. It had been built at Stratford in June 1906 as GER No 558, becoming 7558 under the LNER and renumbered 5456 in the 1946 scheme. *Colour-Rail.com [C Hogg]*

FACING PAGE TOP A Waggon und Maschinenbau (W&M) railbus is alongside a BTH Type 1 in 1964 at Maldon. The railbus was working the 5¾-mile-long Witham-Maldon branch line, which lost its passenger service in September 1964. *www.rail-online.co.uk*

FACING PAGE BOTTOM Waggon und Maschinenbau railbus No E79963 is seen on 5 May 1963 at Witham, from where it would be working the Maldon branch. It had recently undergone a heavy overhaul, during which its original German engine was replaced with an AEC 150hp engine because of the non-availability of spare parts, and it also received dark green livery with yellow warning panels. Incredibly, four out of the five W&M railbuses survived into preservation, where they have all spent much longer in working for their new owners than they ever did for British Railways. *www.rail-online.co.uk*

ABOVE GER Holden 'E4' 2-4-0 No 62792 on 9 June 1956 is at Long Melford whilst working a service from its home depot of Cambridge on the Haverhill branch. Just nine days later it would be officially withdrawn after a life of 54 years, and like nearly all the class would be cut up at its birthplace of Stratford. Long Melford, junction for the Bury St Edmunds and Cambridge lines, closed to passengers in March 1967. *Colour-Rail.com*

FACING PAGE TOP Colchester-allocated GER Holden 'J15' 0-6-0 No 65475 was built in 1913 and is seen here arriving at Lavenham in July 1959 on the Bury St Edmunds to Long Melford branch with the passenger service. It may look like just one coach but another was hidden by the slight curve. The line closed to passengers on 10 April 1961 although freight traffic survived between Bury and Lavenham for a further four years. *Colour-Rail.com [G W Powell]*

FACING PAGE BOTTOM Two brand-new Class 312 GE outer suburban EMUs are led by No 312106 on 24 March 1976 at Colchester. The headcode 5Z74 and the word 'Special' on the train indicator suggests they were on trial. The 312s were developed from the successful AM10 units used on the London Midland Region, the main distinguishing feature being the flat windscreens instead of the wrap-around type on the earlier LMR sets. *www.rail-online.co.uk*

ABOVE With its original 'speed whiskers' and only half of the headcode box working, Cravens two-car DMU No E51277 is about to depart from St Botolphs on 15 November 1959 working the short shuttle service to Brightlingsea. These units became Class 105 and a few lasted until the early 1990s, although most were withdrawn in the early 1980s. *www.rail-online.co.uk*

ABOVE EMU No 140 is at St Botolph's in the mid-1970s. This was one of the BR standard design GE outer suburban four-car units introduced in 1961 – originally known as the Southend Augmentation Stock but becoming more widely used over the network in later years. Classed as '308/1' under TOPS, by the mid-1980s all had been refurbished and repainted in blue/grey. In this photograph the route indicator is no longer in use and has been set to four white blanks. St Botolph's is on a short spur off the Colchester to Clacton line; trains left the main line to stop at its terminus platforms and then reversed out to continue their journey. It has since been renamed Colchester Town because it is nearer to the town centre than Colchester station on the Norwich main line. *www.rail-online.co.uk*

RIGHT One of the ubiquitous Class 105 Cravens units is seen in April 1963 at Brightlingsea. It was the terminus of a single-line branch which left the Colchester to Clacton line at Wivenhoe and was closed in 1964. *www.rail-online.co.uk*

ABOVE 'AM8' EMU No 134 in early 1963 is on a Clacton service. It was the second set in the batch of 32 GE outer suburban four-car sets, built in January 1961 at BR York workshops. *www.rail-online.co.uk*

FACING PAGE TOP Ilford-bound No 081 on 26 May 1960 is passing Clacton carriage sidings where brand new 'AM5' No 406 is stabled, probably awaiting commissioning. The 'AM5s', later Class 305/1, were three-car units built by BR at York for the Enfield and Chingford services. Unit No 081 was one of three EMUs which took part in the safety visibility tests at Alresford in June 1960, each painted with a full-height yellow panel on the cab front. The results for these panels were good although the extension to the roof tended to merge into the bright sky at the top. The area was more effective if bordered by a dark colour and hence the final style adopted was a horizontal band below the front windows, applied to all locomotives and multiple-units. This was the pattern carried by a Cravens DMU in the tests, the other DMU having the existing cream 'whiskers'. *Colour-Rail.com*

FACING PAGE BOTTOM 'AM9' EMU No 615 on 27 March 1966 is at Clacton-on-Sea alongside 'AM8' unit No 137. In 1962 76 'new generation' EMUs were built by BR York Works for use on the Liverpool Street-Clacton/Walton route. They were based on the contemporary Mark 1 locomotive-hauled stock and were formed into 15 four-car and eight two-car sets; all were gangwayed throughout and designed for 100mph operation. The front end of the power cars was rounded to give a streamlined appearance and they were painted in coaching stock maroon. The two-car sets 601-608 were used for strengthening peak services while four-car units 611-618 included a griddle car and 621-627 were the normal four-car set. The griddle cars ceased to be used in 1980 and were removed from the sets. They became Class 309 and were withdrawn from Great Eastern line operation in January 1994. *Colour-Rail.com*

ABOVE Class 305/2 GE outer suburban four-car unit No 509 is at Thorpe Le Soken with another four-car set in the mid-1970s. Thorpe was immediately before the Clacton and Walton lines split on the route from Colchester. *www.rail-online.co.uk*

LEFT The English Electric Type 3 class pioneer No D6700 is photographed on 16 February 1963 at Clacton on Sea. It was delivered from Vulcan Foundry Works on 2 December 1960 and allocated to Stratford, where it stayed until October 1969. No D6700 was repainted into Standard Blue in June 1969 and renumbered as 37119 in February 1974 and then again in March 1988 to 37350. It is now preserved at the National Railway Museum and has the distinction of never officially being withdrawn. *www.rail-online.co.uk*

Mainline to Ipswich, Harwich and Felixstowe

Stratford received five of the first ten English Electric Type 4s in 1958, Nos D200/2/3/4/5, and these were joined on the GER in 1961 by D201/6/7/8/9 when these were displaced from Finsbury Park by the 'Deltics'. They displaced the 'Britannias' on the more important Norwich services, leaving the Brush Type 2s for the lighter trains. No D209 arrives at Manningtree soon after it was transferred in October 1961. It remained an East Anglian locomotive, being reallocated to Ipswich in April 1966, but disappeared to the LMR in August 1967. Withdrawal came in November 1984. *www.rail-online.co.uk*

FACING PAGE TOP Class 47 No 1757 with a container train passes through the deserted platforms at Manningtree on 31 July 1972. Built as No D1757 in 1964 for the Western Region and allocated to Cardiff Canton, it arrived at Stratford in December 1970 and became 47163 in January 1974. It found fame when repainted with Union Jack flags in 1977 but suffered severe fire damage in an accident on Christmas Eve 1977. No 47163 hit two electric locomotives at Kensal Green while hauling a Willesden-Tilbury Freightliner; it was repaired and reinstated almost two years later. It was to carry three more numbers: 47610 from April 1984, 47823 from April 1989 and finally 47787 from October 1994. *www.rail-online.co.uk*

FACING PAGE BOTTOM Class 40 No 40085 on 24 June 1977 is at Mistley, just outside Manningtree on the Harwich line. It was built in July 1960 as D285 and allocated to York. No 40085 was based at Gateshead when this picture was taken; it was withdrawn in March 1984. In the background is the EDME Limited Malt Extract Works which is still operational today, producing ingredients for the baking, cereal and food industries. *www.rail-online.co.uk*

ABOVE Class 47 No 47170 crosses the Stour at Cattawade, between Manningtree and Ipswich, on 24 May 1978. No 47170 was formerly D1765, renumbered in March 1974 and Stratford-allocated from December 1972. It was named *County of Norfolk* in August 1979 and was subsequently renumbered twice more, as 47582 in February 1981 and 47733 in April 1995. *www.rail-online.co.uk*

English Electric Type 3 No D6702 in May 1966 is at Harwich 'Parkeston Qy', as the striplight sign says. The Type 3s ran right through to Manchester Piccadilly on the boat train service from Harwich. No D6702 was a Stratford locomotive from new in December 1960 until September 1967. It became No 37002 in 1974 and subsequently No 37351 in 1989.

www.rail-online.co.uk

FACING PAGE TOP Brush Type 2 No 5525 arrives at Harwich Parkeston Quay on 26 August 1971 with the 09.40 from Liverpool Street. It was renumbered as 31107 in 1974, and was allocated to Stratford at the date of this picture. The impressive original combined station building and hotel built in 1883 is still in existence although its hotel functions have long been converted to office use. *Paul G Bennett © TOPticl Digital Memories*

FACING PAGE BOTTOM Amidst typical 1970s dereliction at Felixstowe Town, Class 100 Gloucester Railway Carriage & Wagon Company (GRCW) two-car unit No E51115 is seen on 15 August 1978. These units were Gloucester's version of the Derby 'Semi-Lightweight' unit and were distinguished by their 'pinched-in' lower body with no separate underframe. They were deemed non-standard and hence not included in the DMU refurbishment programme and were withdrawn in the 1980s. This unit was originally based in Scotland. The headcode box has been plated over. In the 1960s Felixstowe Docks expanded, and passenger trains competed for use of the line with Freightliner services from 1967. In the 1970s the direct line to the docks was reopened and all the sidings were removed, leaving a single line running into the station using Platform 2. *www.rail-online.co.uk*

ABOVE A Class 47 in the very plain mid-1970s blue livery, No 47313 is seen on 2 August 1978 at Elmswell, east of Bury St Edmunds, with a train from Harwich made up of continental ferry wagons. The first are low-sided wagons, almost certainly Belgian or German in origin. The French had similar wagons but the stakes on them were pivotable and so would normally be folded down when not required. The others had stakes that had to be bodily removed from sockets, then stowed, so tended to be left in-situ. They were very versatile and capable of carrying a wide range of goods but are most likely to be carrying heavy steel bar, rather than being empty as they first appear. Built as D1794 in December 1964 and first allocated to Tinsley, 47313 moved to Thornaby in October 1977 and Stratford in January 1982. *www.rail-online.co.uk*

Ipswich and Suffolk branches

ABOVE 'B17/6' 4-6-0 No 61672 *West Ham United* with a down milk empties train in April 1954 takes water at Ipswich. *West Ham United* was a well travelled engine; it arrived from Gorton for the second time in December 1946 and stayed in this area, being allocated to seven sheds until withdrawn in the spring of 1960 only to be cut up at Stratford. It would disappear into Doncaster Works for a replacement boiler four months after this photo was taken. *Colour-Rail.com [J Davenport]*

FACING PAGE TOP Gateshead-allocated Class 40 No 40086 emerges from the tunnel at the south end of Ipswich station with a freight from Harwich and Parkeston Quay on 11 July 1977. A continental ferry van leads the train. Built in 1960 as No D286 and renumbered in 1974, it was always based on the North Eastern Region until the last two years before withdrawal when it moved to the London Midland at Longsight. *www.rail-online.co.uk*

FACING PAGE BOTTOM '03' shunter No 03196 on 12 September 1977 is at Ipswich whilst performing a trip working between the Ipswich yards. Built as No D2196 in August 1961 and new to Swindon, it was on the Southern Region from December 1967 until its transfer to Colchester in October 1975; it was renumbered in March 1974. The match truck was semi-permanently coupled and was supplied not for the shunter to ride on, as on the GWR and BR(W), but to activate the signalling train detection circuits because the short-wheelbase '03s' were not guaranteed to activate all the circuits when running solo. *www.rail-online.co.uk*

LEFT A rather tired-looking Ipswich-allocated 'J15' 0-6-0, No 65389, shunts the daily goods on 11 February 1960 at Framlingham. The LNER 'Toad' brake van has been positioned on the loop and the outgoing train will be assembled against it. The yard crane is painted in BR(E) blue and demonstrates well the faded appearance this paint quickly degraded to. By 13 March 65389, which here sports a tarpaulin weather sheet between tender and cab, had been reallocated to (or was it dumped at?) Parkeston shed, which clearly did not appreciate it as it was withdrawn a month later. The Framlingham branch was a six-mile-long single-track line that ran from Wickham Market on the East Suffolk Line via three intermediate stations at Parham, Hacheston Halt and Marlesford. It opened in 1859 and closed to passengers in 1952 and to freight in 1963. *Colour-Rail.com [J R Besley]*

ABOVE Metro Cammell two-car 'Lightweight' DMU, No E79066, is seen on 10 September 1966 at Aldeburgh. These were the first BR railcars ordered from an outside contractor, although their specification was broadly similar to the Derby units. They were readily identifiable from the later 'Met-Cams' by the cowling below the bufferbeam and the four marker lights. They were deemed non-standard, being compatible only with 'Derby Lightweights', and were withdrawn by mid-1969. The 8½-mile-long Aldeburgh branch ran from Saxmundham on the East Suffolk main line. DMUs took over in June 1956, and journeys were extended to start and terminate at Ipswich. Aldeburgh lost its goods service in November 1959. The construction of the Sizewell 'A' nuclear power station, which opened in 1966, had allowed a five-year stay of execution, but despite economies such as paytrains the line closed to passengers on 12 September 1966. *Colour-Rail.com*

Beccles, Oulton Broad, Lowestoft and Yarmouth

ABOVE Brush Type 2 No D5504 is photographed on 19 July 1958 at Beccles. It was new to Stratford the previous January, became No 31004 in 1974 and was withdrawn in October 1980. Beccles was the junction for the lines to Yarmouth, Lowestoft and the Waveney Valley to Tivetshall which had closed to passengers in 1954 and was shut completely in 1963. *Colour-Rail.com*

FACING PAGE TOP GER Holden 'J17' 0-6-0 No 65558 in July 1957 is at Hopton-on-Sea, which was six miles south of Yarmouth on the Yarmouth-Lowestoft line. It was a local engine, allocated to Lowestoft from summer 1951, and withdrawn from there in January 1960. The sign on the bridge says 'STRAIGHT ON FOR THE CONSTITUTIONAL HOLIDAY CAMP AND

BEACH CLUB, THE EAST COAST LUXURY CAMP. 29 acres alongside the sea. All kinds of sport. Private Beach. Very comfortable modern chalets and beds. Four excellent meals daily.' The absence of cars is noticeable with lots of pedestrian traffic in evidence. *Colour-Rail.com [E Alger]*

FACING PAGE BOTTOM Lowestoft-allocated 'L1' 2-6-4T No 67704 crosses the swing bridge at Oulton Broad in May 1958 with just two coaches forming the Beccles service. New to traffic in March 1948, it was an East Anglian locomotive from May 1950 to January 1959, its only other allocation being to Stratford for the first and last years of its life. No 67704 succumbed in November 1960 only to return to Darlington, its birth place, for cutting in February of the following year. *Colour-Rail.com [E Alger]*

LEFT Brush Type 2 No D5505 departs from Lowestoft Central in May 1958 with a train composed almost entirely of ex-LNER stock, including one which appears to be in new maroon livery. The locomotive went new to Stratford in February 1958, became 31005 in 1974 and was withdrawn in February 1980. The station is the terminus of the 'Wherry Line' from Norwich and the East Suffolk Line from Ipswich, and is the easternmost station on the national rail network. It was also the terminus for the Great Yarmouth service and after closure of that line in 1970 the rails into Platform 1 were removed to form part of the car park. The station building was redeveloped in 1992. *Colour-Rail.com [E Alger]*

ABOVE 'D16/3' No 62613 is seen on 13 July 1957 at Gorleston Camp. One of Yarmouth's long term 'D16/2s', its last two unhappy years would be spent at Peterborough Spital Bridge and March before being withdrawn in October 1960. Gorleston was on the line between Great Yarmouth and Lowestoft which closed in 1970. In the fifties it was a popular holiday resort. In addition to the Gorleston Super Holiday Camp which remained open until 1973, there were lots of boarding houses and hotels and many private houses in the town which took in holiday makers.
Colour-Rail.com [A Payne]

ABOVE 'D16/3' 4-40 No 62546 *Claud Hamilton* in May 1956 at Yarmouth South Town, its home since 1947. It was the only named member of the class, and indeed of any GER locomotive, and would be withdrawn in June of the following year, moving to Stratford for the last time. The nameplate survives in the National Collection. *Colour-Rail.com [Bruce Chapman]*

FACING PAGE TOP 'B17/1' class No 61638 *Melton Hall* is seen after arrival at Yarmouth Vauxhall station in August 1957. A March-allocated engine, it went into Doncaster Works on 10 March 1958 and was condemned. This was when holidaymakers still travelled by train. The group on the left are anxiously checking the departure board as, in the background, the next lot arrive to take their place. *Colour-Rail.com [E Alger]*

FACING PAGE BOTTOM On 18 June 1977 Class 25 pair Nos 25217 and 25117 arrive at Yarmouth Vauxhall with a Saturday excursion from the Midlands. No 25217 was No D7567 until April 1974 and No 25117 was No D5267 until February 1974; both were allocated to the D16 Nottingham Division. Yarmouth Vauxhall is now the sole surviving station at what was once a holiday resort with three stations. It was damaged in World War 2 and finally rebuilt in 1960. The station, with its long curving platforms designed to cater for the holiday traffic during the summer months, was adjoined by extensive freight sidings. *www.rail-online.co.uk*

Norwich and Cromer

'Britannia' Pacific No 70007 *Coeur-de-Lion* is photographed at Norwich in September 1958. One of the original batch allocated to Stratford, it was transferred to March in November 1961 and after storage in October/November 1963 it went to Carlisle Kingmoor in December 1963. The two DMUs and the English Electric Type 4 in the background show that dieselisation of the GE was under way. Indeed, the 204hp Drewry shunters, which later would become so associated with the Norwich scene, had already started to be delivered to nearby Cambridge, and Norwich depot would receive its first example just two months later.
R E Vincent/Transport Treasury

FACING PAGE TOP Gresley 'J39' 0-6-0 No 64900 shunts at Norwich Thorpe Junction signalbox in July 1958. Apart from its initial allocation to Doncaster from new to 1936, No 64900 was always an East Anglian engine, being allocated at various times to Ipswich, Yarmouth, Melton Constable and Norwich from 1955, from where it was withdrawn in July 1959 exactly a year after this photograph. The train is an interesting mix: an ex-LMS Stanier full brake, a tank wagon which is possibly a gas holder vehicle and then a string of fitted vans, several of which have had repairs to their roofs. The PW sidings behind hold such delights as an elderly Pullman coach, now painted black and in departmental service, probably as messing accommodation. *R E Vincent/Transport Treasury*

FACING PAGE BOTTOM Hunslet 204hp diesel-mechanical 0-6-0 No D2567 on 18 March 1962 is at Norwich with Brush Type 2 No D5556 behind. Built at Leeds and new to Norwich in August 1957 as No 11170, it was renumbered in October 1958. It was transferred away to Springs Branch in September 1966 although it may not have worked from there because this depot was used as a sales site for locomotives offered for further industrial service. The bitter winds from the east have resulted in the local fitters reducing the size of the radiator, a practice continued with the '03s'. *www.rail-online.co.uk*

ABOVE Birmingham RCW Class 104 No E50571 is seen on 18 June 1977 at Norwich. These were successful low-density units, some of which survived until the 1990s despite not being included in the 1974 refurbishment programme. Incredibly, these units were occasionally used on through services to Birmingham in the mid-1970s. The journey was slow and excruciating, but not as bad as on a Cravens unit, which was also occasionally used. The headcode box has been replaced by crude welding in a new front centre panel, the paintwork around it showing through. *www.rail-online.co.uk*

ABOVE No 47164, seen on 18 June 1977 at Norwich, was one of two Stratford Class 47s painted with a large Union Jack flag to celebrate the Queen's Silver Jubilee in 1977; No 47163 was the other one. Built as No D1758 in 1964, it became No 47164 in December 1973. It arrived on the GE at March in January 1965, moving to Stratford in April 1966 but left for Tinsley and then Thornaby before returning in January 1970.
www.rail-online.co.uk

FACING PAGE TOP No 03084, formerly D2084 built at Doncaster in 1959, was originally a Southern Region locomotive until transferred in October 1975 to Norwich, where it is pictured on 18 June 1977. It worked there until July 1987 and was then saved for preservation. It was restored to running order in 2003 from scrap condition. It is seen here dual braked and retains the high-level air pipes fitted for running with Southern Region EMUs on Weymouth Quay. The shunter's truck coupled to the 'O3' was needed to operate the track circuits because the locomotive wheelbase was so short.
www.rail-online.co.uk

FACING PAGE BOTTOM A Cravens 105 DMU is photographed around 1970 at Cromer. The livery is a rare example in plain blue with an enlarged yellow panel rather than a full yellow end. Cromer is one of only two former M&GNJR stations to remain operational on the national network, the other being the neighbouring West Runton. It survived because of its location near to the town centre and the beach. It was originally known as 'Cromer Beach' and was renamed plain 'Cromer' in October 1969.
www.rail-online.co.uk

Midland & Great Northern Joint

ABOVE If there is one part of the country that will always be associated with the LMS-designed Ivatt '4MT' 2-6-0s, it is the area served by the former M&GN Joint Railway in East Anglia. The motive power on the line was transformed virtually overnight when over 50 'Doodlebugs' arrived there between September 1950 and September 1952. Ivatt '4MT' 2-6-0 No 43147 waits at Caister Camp Halt in July 1957. Allocated to Melton Constable from new in October 1951, on closure of the M&GN in 1959 it moved to Boston and then to New England in January 1964, from where it was withdrawn the following December. One of the earliest holiday camps was the Caister Camp, which started in 1906. It was originally opened by John Fletcher Dodd as the 'Caister Socialist Holiday Camp'. Accommodation was in tents and the campers helped out with the chores. After World War 1, chalets replaced the tents. By 1951 it could accommodate 800 in chalets and huts, all with cold running water. It was situated right on the beach and had over 90 acres of land. The station was opened in July 1933, one of seven halts for the holiday camp traffic. Caister Camp was the only one with a normal height platform. *Colour-Rail.com [E Alger]*

RIGHT Holden GER 'J17' 0-6-0 No 65581 is shunting at Aylsham Town in June 1958. Allocated to Yarmouth Beach from 1945, No 65581 moved on to Norwich in May 1959. The crossing loop at Aylsham Town could hold 15-coach trains. Note the braced girder footbridge and the Lynn & Fakenham Railway-typ waiting shelter on the left. The tall signalbox on the near right had 21 steps and on summer Saturdays a porter was deployed to help the signalman with the tablet exchanges. *Colour-Rail.com*

FACING PAGE TOP Gresley 'N7' 0-6-2T No 69694 fills its tanks at South Lynn in 1958. Behind it is the through Birmingham to Yarmouth train, known to all on the M&GN as 'The Leicester', which also carried through coaches for Cromer and Norwich. The first coach is a LNER buffet car which, like the engine, only went as far as Leicester, where they were prepared for the return working. During the week the buffet came off at South Lynn but from Friday to Monday it worked to Yarmouth. South Lynn was the focal point for the M&GN freight operations and its two yards, suitably labelled East and West, each dealt with and remarshalled nearly 20 trains every day including trip workings to and from the Great Eastern at nearby King's Lynn. The shed's Ivatt '4MTs' did partake fully in the engine changing ritual on the through passenger services, working both eastwards to Yarmouth and westwards to Peterborough and onto the Midland to Nottingham. The 'N7' was well travelled, and had been allocated to no less than 13 different sheds since the war broke out, even making it to the West Riding District. The ex-GER shed at King's Lynn was its home from March 1958 for over two years. *Colour-Rail.com [J Cramp]*

FACING PAGE BOTTOM Ivatt '4MT' 2-6-0 No 43060 is at Spalding Town in February 1959, the last month of the M&GN. No 43060 has a 40F plate - it was reallocated from New England on transfer of Spalding to the Boston district in June 1958. Although the M&GN 'main' line ran from Peterborough to Yarmouth, an important section was the line that branched off from it at Sutton Bridge and ran for 30 miles via Spalding and Bourne to Little Bytham Junction, where it met the ex-Midland railway line from Saxby, thus forming the link for the traffic to and from the Midlands.

At Spalding there were important connections to the ex-Great Northern Peterborough-Boston and the ex-Great Northern and Great Eastern Joint March-Doncaster lines. The small ex-Great Northern two track shed usually had around seven or eight New England '4MTs' based there at any one time to cover the five diagrams for which it used the 2-6-0s. It had one diagram to Nottingham but apart from that its '4MTs' did not stray very far from home. The short distances worked were due in no small part to the reversals necessary for passenger trains at Spalding.

ABOVE BTH Type 1 No D8206 is photographed on 27 May 1961 at Whitwell & Reepham. It was built by the Yorkshire Engine Company in May 1958 and allocated to Devons Road. D8206 moved to Norwich in December 1959 and remained there until June 1961, when it was transferred to Ipswich. Its final move was to Stratford in June 1962 and it was withdrawn from there in September 1968 soon after becoming Class 15 under TOPS. Whitwell & Reepham served a very agricultural area and suffered against the competition from the nearby GE station. The footbridge had been replaced in 1930 with an ex-Norfolk & Suffolk Joint one from Felbrigg Woods. The station was closed to passengers on 1 March 1959 and was closed completely in May 1964, the signalbox staying open until December 1966. The track remained in use until 1985 to facilitate concrete product movements from Lenwade; this involved the construction of the Themelthorpe Curve west of Reepham linking the Wroxham-County School line with that from Norwich to Melton Constable. Once concrete production ceased, there was no reason to keep the line open and so it was closed. *Colour-Rail.com*

Dereham and Thetford

ABOVE GER Holden 'J17' 0-6-0 No 65567 is seen on 31 March 1962 at Dereham while working the RCTS 'Great Eastern Commemorative Steam Rail Tour' from Liverpool Street, which it took over at Norwich Victoria to Dereham, County School, Swaffham and Thetford, handing back to 'Britannia' No 70003 for the return to Liverpool Street. Five months later No 65567 would be preserved. In the background is the Crisps Maltings, a Grade Two listed building, the current state of which has led to it being placed on the buildings at risk register. *www.rail-online.co.uk*

FACING PAGE TOP 'Britannia' Pacific No 70003 *John Bunyan* waits at Thetford to take over the RCTS Great Eastern Commemorative Steam Rail Tour from 'J17' No 65567 on 31 March 1962 for the journey back to Liverpool Street via Ely, Cambridge and Bishops Stortford. No 70003 was allocated to Stratford from new in March 1951. It moved to Norwich

with the other Stratford 'Britannias' in February 1959 because of a chronic shortage of maintenance staff in London, and to March in June 1961, where it was stored for 10 weeks at the end of 1963 before transfer to the LMR at Carlisle Kingmoor. *www.rail-online.co.uk*

FACING PAGE BOTTOM GER Holden 'J15' 0-6-0 No 65469 from Norwich is at Thetford on 11 June 1960 on a Railway Club excursion using three LMS and two BR brake vans. It ran from Thetford to Bury St Edmunds, and was probably the final passenger train over that line, which closed on 27 June. Thetford was once also the terminus for a branch to Swaffham. The line was closed in 1964 under the Beeching Axe. The other branch ran south to Bury St Edmunds, calling at the town's other station, Thetford Bridge, which had closed to passengers in 1953.
R E Vincent/Transport Treasury

March and Whitemoor

ABOVE 'B2' 4-6-0 No 61639 *Norwich City* is seen in 1958 at March. Rebuilt from a 'B17' at Darlington in 1946, it had always been a local engine, being initially allocated to Norwich then Parkeston, Stratford, Colchester and finally Cambridge in October 1956. No 61639 was withdrawn in May 1959 and cut-up at Stratford. *Norwich City* was the only footballer 'B2' and the club colours of canary yellow and green are evident on the splasher. It is seen here paired with a second-hand NER tender. *www.rail-online.co.uk*

FACING PAGE TOP 'D16/3' 4-4-0 No 62589 at March is photographed in front of the coaling stage in around 1959. It was built as GER No 1819 in June 1910, became LNER No 8819 at the Grouping and No 2589 under the 1946 renumbering. It was converted to 'D16/3' in March 1947 and was withdrawn in May 1959 from March, where it had been allocated since 1942. *www.rail-online.co.uk*

FACING PAGE BOTTOM Thompson 'B1' 4-6-0 No 61026 *Ourebi* is photographed at March on 15 April 1962. A Lincoln-allocated engine in 1962, it had just completed a General repair at Doncaster Plant, only being released to traffic three days earlier. *Ourebi* was another name for the straight-horned antelope Oribi, which name was on sister engine No 61014, so two 'B1s' had inadvertently been named after the same animal. No 61026 was built at Darlington in April 1947 and withdrawn in February 1966. *www.rail-online.co.uk*

LEFT 'Austerity' 2-8-0 No 90037 is seen with a train of 16-ton mineral wagons in the late 1950s at Twenty Foot River Goods station approaching March Whitemoor yard. Built as War Department (WD) No 77422 and originally sent to Eastfield in January 1944, it became LNER No 3037 in February 1947, BR No 63037 in May 1948 and finally No 90037 in October 1950. No 90037 was reallocated from Colwick to Doncaster from February 1960 and in December 1965 it was transferred to Immingham. The up loaded mineral train is unusually short for coal heading for Whitemoor hump yard, where the 'WD' will drop off and the coal wagons will be sorted according to final destination, most of it no doubt heading for the capital. Prior to February 1960 the locomotive was at Colwick and by then the 'LMR takeover' was coming into effect which reduced coal flows to Whitemoor, sometimes resulting in shorter trains like that shown here. That wouldn't have been the case with down empties, which tended to run in blocks of 60 or more, depending on the length limit (60 to Worksop, Doncaster and Colwick, 75 to Mansfield Concentration Depot). *www.rail-online.co.uk*

ABOVE '9F' 2-10-0 No 92184 is seen on 16 June 1963 at March. Only the second production '9F' to be built with a double chimney, No 92184 was transferred from its original shed of New England to Colwick in June 1963 shortly after this picture was taken. It is paired with a BR1F tender carrying 7 tons of coal and 5700 gallons of water. No 92184 was fitted with AWS during a Light Intermediate works visit at Darlington in April/May 1960 and was withdrawn in February 1965 after a working life of only seven years. *www.rail-online.co.uk*

LEFT English Electric Type 3 No D6748 is at Whitemoor in 1964 in charge of a Class 3 parcels train coming from the Wisbech/King's Lynn direction and heading for March station. It went new to Tinsley in August 1962, moved to Stratford June 1967 and left for Healey Mills in October 1969. It was renumbered as No 37048 in March 1974. The lines in the left foreground lead to Peterborough (now a single track!). Those in the distance through the two double slips feed to the depot, the ones beyond through the double junction lead to the yards and then to Spalding via the GN&GE Joint lines. The signalbox is Whitemoor Junction which survived into the 1990s. *www.rail-online.co.uk*

ABOVE Brush Type 2 No D5582 in 1964 at March heads an unusual procession of diesel and steam engines, all manned and in steam. They will either head off for the station to take over incoming freights, or will set back into the yards. In the background another Brush Type 2 with a freight from Wisbech waits to pass by Whitemoor Junction box. The Brush Type 2 spent its first few years in East Anglia, initially at Norwich before moving to March in September 1961 and then in April 1966 to Immingham. It received its TOPS number 31164 in February 1974. *www.rail-online.co.uk*

Peterborough and New England

ABOVE GNR 'J6' 0-6-0 No 64219 is photographed at New England. It was fresh from a General repair at Doncaster in September 1958 where even the worksplate was polished (no over-painting of pre-Grouping plates at 'The Plant', unlike LMR works). The Lincoln-allocated 'J6' had worked down over the GN&GE Joint line as far as Spalding, then over to New England as seen here. The 'J6s' worked extensively on all types of traffic including express passenger on the M&GN until displaced by the Ivatt 'Flying Pigs', after which they were reallocated to such locations as Boston and Colwick. *www.rail-online.co.uk*

RIGHT Ivatt '4MT' 2-6-0 43082 has two coaches in tow on the former Midland Line from Stamford at Peterborough in June 1963. It had been repainted at Horwich with short lining and small cab numbers during a General repair from 15 March to 25 April 1963. It was transferred away from New England in November to Barrow Hill and ended up at Langwith Junction in late 1965, although probably only as a paper transfer prior to withdrawal. *www.rail-online.co.uk*

LEFT Brush Type 4 No D1531 stands in front of the coaling stage at New England in 1963. It was delivered new to Finsbury Park in July 1963 but two months later moved to Sheffield, initially at Darnall until Tinsley was completed. It was renumbered in May 1974 as No 47424 and was withdrawn in 1992. *www.rail-online.co.uk*

BELOW English Electric Type 4 No D264 on 11 February 1968 is at Peterborough New England shed with Nos D5621, D1765 and D6589. The latter was a very unusual visitor, probably because it had been declared a failure on the daily York cement train. No D264 was originally a Haymarket engine without train indicator panels. It remained there until September 1981, when it moved to Longsight before withdrawal in April 1982. It became No 40064 in October 1973. *www.rail-online.co.uk*